Journey Into Darkness

Pedro Ramirez

Published by

Copyright © 2018 by Pedro Ramirez

All rights reserved.

ISBN: 978-0-9827408-9-7

In loving memory of Marco Antonio Nungaray.

You will always be loved and you will be missed. Thank you for the memories. I can't wait to see you in Heaven; I long for that moment.

May you rest in peace, my brother.

March 3, 1986 - November 1, 2017

I dedicate this fight to my family and loved ones, and to everyone in the everyday struggle worldwide.

Editor's Forward

This book is not a conventional story or biography.

It is a journal: the pouring out of the thoughts from a mind in pain, and a spirit fighting to hold fast to thin threads of faith. It may be free-flowing and unstructured in the traditional literary sense. It is important that it is told this way to demonstrate what happens to us (any of us) when our minds are struck by mental illness. It is told as a series of thoughts and emotions, statements and proclamations strung together on a wire of thought. It aims to reflect the layering of whatever sensations are taking place in a mind receovering from psychological injury.

Key to this journal is the theme of pain. Pain can be overwhelming, especially when our foremost line of defense in rationalizing pain is incapacitated: our minds. People suffering from any mental illness which inflicts depression, anxiety, fear, frustration, and hopelessness are robbed of their ability to control how they feel. Our brains do our thinking, and when our brains become sick, our thinking is fundamentally and physically compromised. The power to control and process pain is lost regardless of the will or strength or intelligence of the person. This piece strives to make that very clear.

As human beings, we detest pain and suffering. But in every age, pain has been a part of us. It has never been escaped in full. Pain may also be more than an adversary to us. With pain comes humility, empathy, and a better appreciation for beauty and joy. With pain comes courage, learning to trust, and fortified faith. In pain, there is widsom.

This work, thus, is not all written with a message of misery. It extends a greater message of hope for serenity for anyone suffering from mental illness. The mind that produced this work has traveled through a trench of Hell, wrestled tooth and nail with demons, and made it safely back home with treasures of wisdom and a proclamation that all is well on the other side of the misery.

Mental illness can render us desperately vulnerable, and it is imperative therefore, to walk not alone, but together on the journey into darkness.

Loren John Presley

Contents

Invitation Into the Dark	1
Advice for the Journey	3
Mental Illness	4
Humanity	5
They Don't Make Them Like This No More	7
Wisdom That Comes With Pain	8
As the Illness Tries to Take Me Under	10
Mustard Seed of Faith	16
Doubt and Regret	20
Healing in the Hospital	24
My Silent Screams	29
Sometimes I Wonder	39
Either Let Me Fly or Give Me Death	42
If It Takes for Me to Suffer	54
Im Glad	56
In The Darkest of My Days	58
I See Life a Little Different Now	60
The Reason	62

Courage

"Mental or moral strength to venture, persevere, and withstand danger, fear, or difficulty."

Merriam-Webster Dictionary

Invitation into the Dark

Many days and nights of inner struggle; these things are so raw, so real, so personal, and so uncivilized.

I'm being pulled between the thin border of sanity and insanity.

I've died a thousand deaths, so I do not fear death.

I've hidden long enough. I've suffered many years and shed so many tears. This is a testament of the human spirit, and my own inner-strength.

I pour out my heart and soul in these pages.

I share these things of pain and suffering to anyone who wants to listen.

This is only the beginning of my life.
The mind is so fragile.

Comfort my pain and suffering.

Show me a person who's been through
what I've been through
and I'll show you
one bad motha-fucker.

Todo lo que deseas con el corazon
se hace realidad.

En la vida se puede ganar
o se puede perder.

Mi familia es mi vida.

Advice for the Journey

- Always remember that love is as strong as death.

- Live every day like it was your last.

- Give love and you will get love back, that's for real.

- Love your life until you die.

- Everything your heart desires will come true.

- In life, sometimes you win, and sometimes you lose

- My family is my life.

- When I go as far as I can, Christ takes me the rest of the way.

- The love of God and my family's love keep my dreams in motion.

- I can accept failure. But I won't handle not trying.

Mental Illness

Mental illness is like being dead among the living. Walking, talking, laughing, but dead among the living. Pain becomes constant in your life, never leaving you, endured every second so long as you are awake. It is like being in a room full of people but you still feel alone. You're losing your soul and you're fighting with all your heart to try and find it.

It's a lonely fight.

Mental illness is like losing yourself and not being able to find yourself.

Mental illness is so dark and your trying to find the light, but only darkness remains. It feels like you're the only one hurting and feeling empty inside, not being able to cry. When you do manage to cry, its like crying tears of blood.

Its like being in Hell inside your own mind.

It's like something is eating you up inside, but you don't know what it is.

I wish I could take the pain away.

It's a struggle everyday.

Humanity

Humanity is so weak and fragile. We are only dust. Our days on Earth are like flowers. We bloom and die.

Faith is the only thing that keeps humanity going. Do not underestimate the power of the human spirit. It can overcome great difficulties if people just believe.

There has to be a love for life in order to maintain oneself in it. Though the human spirit is strong, the human mind is such a delicate thing. How can someone's mind make a person think that life is not worth living?

But humanity keeps going because God loves every one of us.

So while life is fleeting, I have to live my life like there's one more move to make.

Pronto llegara el dia de mi puerte te lo juro por mi gente que un dia illegara.

There is nothing to fear but fear itself.

List for my Life

Today

Take Marcus to a Laker's basketball game.

This week

Go to work.

Go to church every Sunday.

So long as I live

Have faith in God's plan.

They Don't Make Them like this No More

They don't make them like this no more
Real to the core.
Big heart, but built for war.

Don't make the mistake to take my kindness for weakness.
Listen to what I believe in,
Even if what I believe in stops me from breathin'.

Wisdom that Comes with Pain

When you see someone and are tempted to think, "Wow, they got power," just say to yourself, "Fuck them! I got power. Why? Because I got family!"

My family is my life.

People who put up a mask will eventually be unmasked. Yeah, everbody wears a mask but how long will it last?

Just walking in the streets, death could take you away. You're never guaranteed that you'll live to see the next day.

Live every day like if it was your last.

The truth will set you free. The less you have to lie to yourself or anybody else, the better off you are.

We each have a star. All we have to do is find it. Once you do, everyone who sees it will be blinded.

Nobody in this world is perfect by a long shot.

Wisdom that Comes with Pain

Do not worship money. What good is it for a person to gain the world, but lose their soul in the process? I wonder! What good will all the money in the world do you if you cannot enjoy it with loves ones?

To live is to suffer, but you have to keep going on no matter what. There will be a time when you shine as bright as the stars.

Think before you speak.

Be careful of the ones who always want to get you high cause when the time comes that one will let you die.

Do the right thing, cause after the tears come the cheers.

Remember that nobody in the world can change you. You have to want to change yourself for the better. Always be yourself, like they say. Keep it real.

You gotta think about loyalty first. You got loyalty, money will come. Keep it real with your loved ones, money will come. If you don't realize that, your got a lot to learn.

In my heart I mean well. As time goes by what I have in my heart will begin to show. And when I get going on my journey, I'm not looking back for nothing cause I'll know where I'm headed.

I'm so tired of the suffering, but I just gotta keep remembering everything I know is right. What I know makes sense.

Be careful of those who want to be you; they smile but are not really happy when they see you.

As the Illness Tries to Take Me Under
An open-hearted prayer to God

God, this is how I really feel at this moment. Just give me the strength to keep going on no matter what.

So much pain, sometimes I think to myself, "Is it worth it?"

This mental illness that I have inside of me is such a horrible illness. I wonder to myself how cruel life is when you live with such an illness.

Why do these devasting illnesses even exist? I mean, life is hard enough as it is and to top it all off I have to live with such a bullshit illness like this. I mean, I get so mad at this illness sometimes that I get in front of the mirror and I start cursing the shit out of it. Life can't get any worse than this. But I know what keeps me going is that little faith I have inside of me that hopes one day I will wake up and You will cure me completely, and I can lead normal life. The most important thing that keeps me going with me in this world is my family and loved ones, whom I love so much.

I have lost a lot of faith against this illness, to be honest. I've been fighting this illness for far too long and its seems hopeless sometimes. I've been taking anti-depressants and going to my doctor but nothing seems to work. At this moment I feel like this illness has cut my life short and now I have to live with such darkness inside my own self.

It's like being in Hell of Earth.

As the Illness Tries to Take Me Under

I feel there is nothing worse than having a mental illness like this and not being able to snap out of it.

I wouldn't wish this illness upon my worst enemy.

As a matter of fact I wish things like this didn't even exist. Things like this cause too much pain to the person, to the family who loves them and all the people who really care and love that person. Sometimes I wonder why did You create me if I was doomed to live in misery? Living with this illness is just too much.

I sometimes feel like screaming at the top of my lungs but I know its not going to accomplish anything.

The worst feeling in the world is hurting so much inside and not being able to do anything about it. There's nowhere to run; nowhere to hide. This illness makes me feel like taking my own life is the only way out. It makes me feel like I will never see the light unless I choose death over life. I choose life because no matter how much pain I feel inside, it is nothing to the pain I will cause my family and friends who really care about me would go through, if I choose the path of ending my life.

Mi familia es mi vida.

There are times when I think I am stupid for putting my mind, body, and soul through all this pain. Or does it show how much inner strength I posses inside my own heart?

The only time that my whole being is totally at ease is when I fall asleep at night. I know that every living person is afraid of death. But sometimes I wonder if being dead is the same as being asleep, because when we are asleep all the pain and suffering seem to go away at least for the night.

If that is the case, then all we are so afraid of is just an eternal sleep.

These are just my inner most thoughts as this illness tries to take me under.

I really hate it when they tell me to just snap out of it like if it were that simple. How could they say that if they have never even been in my shoes?

I wish I were not in my own shoes because its too painful. I hate waking up in the morning to the same old bullshit illness that unfortunately I have to live with every day. Every day is the same thing, waking up feeling like I have no purpose in this life.

Physically, I feel like a one-hundred-year-old man because I get exhausted so easily and the bottom of my feet hurt. Emotionally, I am totally worn out from fighting this illness every waking second.

My faith is totally devastated because I see no way out of it and I have lost a lot of faith that I will ever recover from this illness. I feel as though I will have to live with this forever.

Another thing I hate from this whole situation is the pain that my poor mother, whom I love so much, has to go through everyday that I tell her that I'm not feeling any better.

Everyone tells me that I don't look sick. Even when I see myself in the mirror I don't see a sick person. I see a totally healthy person, but that's not how I feel inside. Inside I am struggling every second of my life with my own thoughts.

As the Illness Tries to Take Me Under

But I know that everything this illness tells me is a lie because this illness tells me that I never was a happy person. But I know that is nothing but a lie because I was once a kid and I enjoyed life to the fullest. There are some things I don't understand like, "Why would God let anyone go through this insanity?" I guess its going to take the man in me to conquer this insanity.

God, why did you even give me life if it was going to be cut short by living with this awful illness? I really believe that I will have to learn to live with the worst pain in the world if I plan to keep going on in this crazy life. But I really can't see myself living too much longer with all this pain.

It seems to me as if this illness is killing me slowly inside.

I really don't know where to go from here because I don't see the end of this from where I stand.

I sometimes wish You would take my life in my own sleep, so I can rest in peace and not be in pain internally. Dear God, why don't you end this insanity I have to go through every waking moment of my life?

This bullshit illness is just too much! It takes everything out of you. It totally handicaps you and that's what really sucks.

I feel that I can't go to to work at this moment because I don't feel well at all. The medication I'm taking, I feel, is not doing anything to make me better.

Life is like a heavy load that I can't get rid of. I sometimes wish that You would give me the mind of a ten-year-old instead of having this horrible illness. I wish that I was retarded but not feel this awful pain.

Sometimes I feel as if life is just me against the world with nothing to lose.

I feel like a slave with nothing to gain against this illness.

I feel like my life was cut short because I will never be able to fall in love, never have a baby to call my own, never be able to buy a house. I will never be able to enjoy the holidays with my family.

I feel like I'm trapped inside a maze and can't find my way out. Oh Lord, I've sufffered for so long and shed so many tears.

I've fallen to the ground on my knees so many times shedding tears and praying to You. What do you want from me, God? What must I do to free myself from this prison I live in everyday? I guess that in a perfect world I would have never caught this illness, but the game of life is a totally different story.

All these crazy days and crazy nights...

How long will it last? I just don't know. Though things change and things happen for a better future. That's what I keep telling myself. I keep telling myself, there is still a future inside of me.

And I'm not just telling this to myself alone. The unconditional love of my family and friends keeps me going on in this craziness I go through.

Still, it's a fight. I feel trapped in this prison of insanity. When will it end? What does the future hold for me? I really can't tell because I really can't see the future, especially in my condition.

As the Illness Tries to Take Me Under

I'm almost afraid to fall asleep now because I don't want to wake up the next morning and still feel the same. No matter where I go, I can't hide from this illness and I can't explain to anyone else what a bitch and and awful feeling that is. They just can't imagine what it feels like to see other people laugh and me feeling like I will never be able to laugh like that again.

I can't believe that I survived growing up in some of the worst neighborhoods in Los Angeles. I tried to stay away from gangs, drugs and other dangerous behaviors, all for nothing.

Just to end up with this bullshit illness.

It just seems funny to me and its makes me realize how cruel life can be.

Can anyone stop the pain?

Sometimes I wish I had to a button I could push to completely get rid of the pain and bad thoughts that fill up my head. But that doesn't happen and I have to put up with it and fight it as best I can. If only I could calm the storm and beat this illness. But I know its going to be the hardest fight I will ever have to put up.

God, bless me in my own personal struggle. Just keep that mustard seed of faith that burns inside of me. Keep my faith burning and make the flame grow and grow as the days go by. No matter how bad things get inside my head, life keep going on no matter what...

Mustard Seed of Faith

Today I finally cried because I hadn't cried in a long time. The things that triggered my tears was that I saw my sister's baby and saw how beautiful he was.

My sister hugged me and told me she wanted me to get better.

I realized that no matter how much pain and numbness this illness causes me, I have the unconditional love of my family. Even though this illness tells me I am nohting and makes me feel like crap, I know it is all lies and deceptions. I'm only twenty-five years old. I haven't even begun to live.

Something just tells me, "Keep on going young man; one of these days the storm will clear and you will see the light."

I hope it happens soon because I'm tired of this. I wish that I could wake up one day and it were all a crazy nightmare, but that wont happened because what I feel is so real that sometimes it scares me big time.

———————————————

I went to church today and I wish I was well so I could really enjoy the true experience of going to church.

Mustard Seed of Faith

Today they had a very good concert there. The church and parking lot were both filled up. Everyone had a good time listening to the Imperials; they are a quartet of singers.

That's why I wish I was well because this illness doesn't let me enjoy myself like I know I could otherwise. I hate this illness because it makes me see how everyone is having a good time and I know that I'm just sitting there fighting my illness.

I just need the Holy Spirit to lay His hands upon me and move me in the right direction. I sometimes believe that the little faith I have is enough to completely heal myself from this terrible illness.

I put my life in the hands of God, because I feel like I've reached the end of the road. Another cloudy day. Oh my God, when will You ever let me see the light? When will the rain clear up?

I feel ike I'm running a race that I will never be able to finish. Like I'm climbing a mountain that keeps going on forever and I can't see the top of it from down here. Another day gone by and I'm afraid to fall asleep because tomorrow is going to be the same thing.

I realize that I will need to finished the race no matter what, because I have a family who needs me and really cares about me. I don't know how much my heart can take, but as long as I keep waking up in the morning, I will keep on going.

Can anyone help me out of my struggle?

The thing that bothers me the most from this is that I keep going to the doctors and, as before, they say I'm in perfect physical condition. It is just this illness that won't go way no matter what I do.

One thing is for sure, I can't throw in the towel because the fight is going well into the late rounds. I'm just waiting for the bright shiny day after the rain.

What is it that I must do to beat this illness? The answer to that question is what I'm looking for. I really don't know where the answer lies.

Sometimes the pain gets so bad that I feel like I'm going to explode.

Do anything, God, to take away the pain much faster. I really hate to think like this, but I feel as though I'm going to have to learn to live with pain and it will have live to with me forever.

Sometimes the pain gets so bad that I feel like I'm going to explode.

Do anything, God, to take away the pain much faster. I really hate to think like this, but I feel as though I'm going to have to learn to live with pain and it will have live to with me forever.

Look into my eyes and tell me what it is you see...

I wish I was well so I could go back to work, but I can't in my condition. It drains me out completely, physically, emotionally, and spiritually. I mean, thats the job of the illness: to complete make me feel like I'm handicapped.

Jesse's family keeps coming by to try and cheer me up. He calls me on the phone to see how I'm doing and he takes me to church every Sunday. I thank God for putting him in my life when I really needed somebody to tell me to keep going on.

Mustard Seed of Faith

I hate this illness because everything I worked so hard for I feel has been taken away from me. Right now, there is nothing in the world that has any meaning to me, especially money. I know we need money to live and buy food so we can fill our empty stomachs, but I can't get any satistfaction from anything.

This fight that I am putting up I dedicate to God, my family, and Jesse's family who I don't know what I would do without.

Doubt and Regret

Sometimes I lay back and ask myself why did this happen to me? Is this some type of test that God is putting me through? Even though my faith is cut short, I keep praying anyway because I hope that one day God will listen to my humble prayers.

I sit around outside to get some fresh air everyday and I see the birds play and fly around so happily. It makes me think if had wings I would fly.

Nobody ever said that life was easy, but why does it have to be so hard for me?

———————————————————————

I went to Lerdo Jail today to offer my brother some money.

I hardly like to go out anymore because I see everybody going on with their lives and this illness keeps me from going on with mine. I thought to myself that me and my brother were both in prison except that I'm in a mental prison of my own which I think is worse than being behind bars and four walls. I hate to think about how my mother feels that one of her sons is in jail and one is mentally ill. I bet she spends many sleepless nights crying and praying for both her sons. She doesn't need all that stress and worry in her life but that's how life is; it's very cruel.

Doubt and Regret

I just hope that God doesn't close the gates on me, because life is a heavy load.

When will I ever get to rest from my sickness?

Even though I walk through the valley of the shadow of death everyday, I fear no evil. God, I know that something inside me is dead you just have to give me your attention and bring me back from the dead.

Now I know why a lot of people take their own lives. It is such a struggle to live with so much pain inside and not be able to do anything about it. A living Hell is all I can call this stuggle that I'm going through.

It would be a lie if I told you that I never thought of death. How can I show you how I feel inside? How can I explain how I feel when all I know is pain?

I'd love to go back to when we played as kids, but things change and thats the way it is. Things will never by the same.

Dear God, clear my mind and clear my thoughts so I can feel the way I felt when I was a kid. When I was a kid, we had it rough, but we always had enough.

Right now I have to go to sleep so I can wake up tomorrow and go to church.

Nothing matters to me but my mental health. I so wish that tomorrow I could wake up and feel completely cured. I know a lot of people who would be glad to hear the news that I was completely healed. But I know that tomorrow is going to be the same thing all over again.

I keep telling myself, "God, if you don't want me in this world, why don't you just take me away?"

My mom's tears rolling down her cheeks is what keep me going because I just can't imagine what she would go through if I did something to myself.

I have been fighting for too long and to hard to just give in to this bullshit illness.

I hear on the radio that God cures all kinds of illnesses with miracles. And I wonder to myself why doesn't He grant me a simple miracle, by curing me? Haven't I and my family been through enough pain? What must I do to get God's attention? Hasn't He seen and been there while I've been going through my struggle? I just don't see any way out of this.

This morning my mom and aunt and the kids went to the river and they wanted me to go with them, but I wasn't feeling too good this morning. I felt tired from yesterday playing basketball at Jesse's house. I couldn't get up. I slept all day long. I was laying in bed when my brother, Tavo, came into the room. He asked me how I felt and I told him that I wasn't feeling too good.

Then I started crying uncontrollably, telling my brother that I couldn't take it any more. I started thinking to myself that I couldn't enjoy the day with my family and I told my brother that I felt that was bullshit. How could this illness ruin my life like that?

Doubt and Regret

It just killed me that my brother had to see his big brother crying in front of him and feeling that there is no way out; I was just trapped in a maze. Even my brother realized how much I was hurting inside. I could see the pain in his eyes and in his voice. It's a feeling of hopelessness.

Reality really hit him hard then. He realized that what I talk about is the reality that I'm going through all this.

God, what can I do? Please give me a sign from above that everything is going to be okay. Because at this point, I just don't know where to go from here. Guide me.

Healing in the Hospital

My brother told me that he wished he could take all the pain that I'm feeling. But I told him that there is no way that I would let him take my pain because it is too much pain for anybody to handle. I wouldn't even give this pain to my worst enemy. Because no one in the world should suffer as much as I am suffering inside.

Today was a hard day for me. I had to admit myself into the hospital because I wasn't feeling good at all. I got admitted into Memorial Center about five in the evening. It was hard for me to stay here because I miss my family so much. I started crying when Jesse and I went into my room. I felt so hopeless.

I felt I couldn't do anything to keep myself out of the hospital. I know that Jesse felt bad seeing me like this and having to leave me here by myself. The nurse in here gave me a little hope. They are so helpful and caring. One nurse told me she had been depressed for two years and that she got out of it. I thought to myself how could someone survive all that time with so much pain inside? She kind of let me know that everything was going to be okay; all I had to do was hang in there.

I know that my family cares so much about me. That's what keeps me going too.

Healing in the Hospital

What is it inside of me that makes me feel this way? What can I do to make myself better? I'm too young to let this bullshit illness take complete control of my life. Hopefully inside the hopsital they can find the right type of medication to get me up and at 'em.

My family came to visit me today. I felt pretty good about seeing them here. They really lift my spirits. I see my little brother and sisters run around and play and I wish that some day I can feel like they do. No worries and carefree.

When the visit was over, it really hurt me to see my mom cry when she left, because she cares so much about me.

God, please make me better so I can jump aroud with joy.

Life is really cruel. How could this illness tell you that life is not worth living anymore? How could the mind go into such the deepest, darkest places?

Having thought about this a while, I have really surprised myself by going on as far as I have with so much pain inside. I always say that my mind is controlled by this illness, but it does not control my heart and soul. Those belong to God.

I do put everything in Gods hands because He is the only one who knows what I've been going through. I also really can't imagine myself in this world without my family and Jesse and his family.

I've also talked to some of the people here now and it is crazy because everyone looks normal. But we all have our different problems. I pray for everyone in this hospital to get well at some point in time.

What I really hate is that they have a place for young kids. I really hate to think that young kids have to go though what we are going through as adults.

I guess tomorrow is a whole new day and I have to keep going and keep the faith alive and never give up on this long, long race.

I see things totally different now. As I see people who come in and out of here and as I get to know more of the people I realize that even though we are sick we are all kind and loving people.

I thank God for giving me a family who really loves me and cares for me. I really don't know what I would do without my family.

Why does God let these things happen?

Today was a beautiful day. Too bad I'm not feeling well enough to enjoy it. I at least considered to go out to the park or something and play basketball, however.

I realized today that I have to get well no matter what. I have so much to live for. Even though this illness tells me I have nothing to live for, I know it is all a lie. How could a person who is twenty-five years old feel like there is nothing out there?

While I'm still in the hospital, I know one thing: being here really makes me miss my family. Every time they leave after a visit it makes me cry. I've cried so many tears now because of this illness. The reality is that I will probably have to live with this illness for the rest of my life. Still, I hope that just maybe being in the hospital and taking the right amount of medication will do the trick for me to get better.

Healing in the Hospital

I won't mind living with this illness but I want the pain to diminish to where as I could function out in the world. Because I really don't want to lose my job. I want to get better so I can get on with my life and enjoy all the years I have left.

I know that I've been put in this world for a reason. Right now I don't know what it is, but some day God will let me see the light.

I don't know why all this is happening to me, but deep down inside of me I know there is a reason. I must endure this hardship to become better person. But how much more strength must I show?

Perhaps its not all inner strength. I met some of the best people in the world at Memorial Center who lended me their strength too. I met Matt, Loui, Ruth, and Beating, who we called "B." I will never forget these people. They became like a family in there to me. They gave me hope, which I thought I lost forever. It made me realize that I wasnt the only one going through this tribulation. We all shared our stories and that made a big difference in the way I saw life.

I know that there is still a lot of fighting to be done to beat this illness, but I feel the best thing that ever happened to me while it's hitting me was when I went into Memorial Center. No matter what ever happens to me, I will never forget that experience. I learned the true meaning of love between people and how close people can get in a short period of time.

I came out of the hospital with a feeling of hope and regained my faith. I known I can beat this illness. It's just going to take some time. There is no way I can pay back Jesse and Cindy and their family, but I hope they understand that they are appreciated.

Journey Into Darkness

    Inside my mind I couldn't find a place to rest until I went into Memorial Center and met some of best people in the world. Those people in the hopsital will always be in the my heart.
    We must remember that tomorrow always comes after the dark.

My Silent Screams

I had a good day today. I spent some time playing with my little niece, Jasmin and I enjoyed it.

My family will alwyas be in my heart with undinctional love. Me and my brother took all our little brothers and we went swimmig in the pool. My sister, Cristina, cooked some carne asada and we had a good time.

Somtimes I wonder how many people fall victim to mental illness. May God rest their souls.

It's dark and Hell is hot.

What's going on inside of me? It is just not fair that I felt like I was getting a second wind at trying to beat this illness and all of the sudden I get crushed right back under this illness. That is just not fair, God, to my family, my friends, and especially myself. I felt like I came back from the depths of Hell just to go right back.

How could you let this happen, God? Please shine your light on me. Let me get that hope and faith that I had for that brief period of time.

I'm still hoping that You give the doctors the power to completely heal me or make me feel better. Because, God, I promise you that I'm just not living well with this illnes. I've been taking this pain for far too long.

There just have to be better days in my future. I mean, I've done everything I can do to beat this illness. What else must I do?

Please, God. I beg you to walk by my side so you can see what I'm really going through.

I've kind of learned to live with this illness by now. But I know it can't kill me. I wake up so I must keep going on no matter what. Please let me keep going on in this fight for my life. I mean, I know that there is no reason for me to be ill.

I have my family, my friends, and my church family. They are all my support group. I know that all this illness makes me feel is nothing but lies. I will go on untill this illnes makes me crazy.

I still wish that this was all just a horrible nightmare. But I know that tomorrow it will still be with me.

Hopefully everything will be all right and I am able to keep my sanity. There is no worse feeling in the world than looking at life though the eyes of a mentally ill person.

I just love my family with all my heart and if I did something stupid, it would tear their world apart. I thank you, God, for giving me those couple of days of feeling good and enjoying it with my family. I just don't understand why You would let anyone go through his painful experience. I look at my little brothers and sisters and I see them so happy. I just couldn't do anything to hurt their little hearts.

My Silent Screams

I figure I am a very strong person to live with this illness. Strong as I am, I just feel like I've been cursed by this illness all over again and that's just not fair.

I wish I could take the pain away. How could it be possible that I feel good for a couple of days and all of a sudden just fall deeper into my personal hell? I just don't undertsand how life is so cruel.

Please, God, listen to my prayers and to what I write and heal me. Let me breathe. I feel like I'm under water and I can't catch my breath.

It's just so frutstrating to not be able to do what I have to do to beat this illness. Like I said, God, just keep me going on no matter what happens for the love of Jesus. I feel like I'm walking on shaky ground. Somebody, tell me what did I ever do to deserve this fate.

What's really going on? Where do I go from here? God please lead the way and I will follow. I refuse to give in to this illness. I am so confused I just don't know what to do. What I have is not that bad, but this illness doesn't let me enjoy what I have. The mental pain of this illness is so debilitating that it is just unbelievable.

Tomorrow always comes after the dark and I will be there no matter what. Even though I am tired of frighting ths, I must keep going on no matter what for the love of my family and friends who really care about me. Hopefully some day I will wake up and everything will be better.

Today I saw a boxing match and it was good. I just hate that I can't enjoy a fight like that as I could when I was well.

Why?! Why won't it end? This illness has come back to put me up against the ropes.

I sometimes wonder is my illness uncurable? Will the doctors ever give me the right medication that I need? Will this fight I'm putting up all be in vain? What does the future hold for me? The frustration that I feel is so powerful that I just can't explain it. Why did God give me life if I was going to end up like this? How long will I be able to put up with this horrible pain? I still remember having good times when I was a kid. But this illness makes it feel like I'm a man in pain who was never a boy.

Things will never by the same. That's just the way life is. One life to live and its so hard for me to be positive. The only thing I can rely on at this time is my inner strength not to harm myself.

Another day gone by and I still feel the same.

Why is it so hard to beat this illness? I try, try and try and I will keep trying until something happens. I believe in myself even though this illness wants me to give up. Why do I keep going? I don't know why, but I have to keep going. How do I deal witht his illness and not go crazy?

How could a chemical imbalance make people go through so much hell? I wish there was a sure cure for all these crazy mental illnesses. There are too many people suffering from these illnesses. My God, can't you see how much I am suffereing. Does my fight not mean anything to you?

My Silent Screams

This hasn't been my day, my week, my month or ever my year. It's crazy, but I keep going.

I can't believe that an illness can stop you from looking forward towards the fututre. Sometimes I feel like I am already dead. I may look normal on the outside, but inside I'm going through Hell. I realize that I must fight my own demons or whatever is going on inside of me. I put this illness in God's hands. Like Jesse says, "God is in control."

Why do I feel like everything around me fell to the ground? Imagine how I feel having to wake up in the morning to the same thing everyday. I am a person who is able to withstand immeasurable amount of mental pain. There are so many things for me to experience in this life.

Why do I feel like my life has been cut short?

I know God doesn't like people to take their own lives. But it is crazy because in my head, I've killed myself so many times. I've even pictured myself in a coffin. Maybe I should have been dead a long time ago. Maybe I'm already dead, but only the body remains. I sometimes feel like crawling out of my skin and finding something to hide from this illness. I wonder why I feel this way. It's a tough life to live, but somebody has to live it. I have thought of many ways to end my life! Like walking somewhere out of the house and drinking all my medication. Like renting a car and driving to Tijuana and go off a cliff. Getting in front of a train. Jumping off a fast moving vehicle. Jumping off a building. Buying a gun. Slicing my wrists.

It's crazy what these thoughts can do to a person. Sometimes I wish I had an off button I could push in my body and I would go into an eternal sleep.

God, it's such a great big, universe and here I am trapped inside of myself, confused and full of questions. That's why I have to have the mentality of never, ever giving up no matter what happens. All that I desire is to be able to live a normal life like every human being should. I must dig deep inside myself to find the strength to keep on going forward in this fight.

Tomorrow I have an appointment for both my doctors in the same day, but different times. God I pray that you give the doctors the power and the wisdom to be able to heal me. For all the darkness that I've been through, I never thought that I would see my 26th birthday. After my birthday on October 7th, I'll look forward to being here when the new millenium gets here.

It's not as easy as it seems to carry the weight of this illness. I can't understand why it's been so long, but I've been combating this illness and I don't feel like I'm making any progress.

For people who don't think that I'm going through Hell, I say, "If only you could see what I see, do what I do, and feel what I feel. Walk in my shoes, then you'll hurt your feet."

For me right now, I feel like I'm just trying to survive the day so I can go to sleep at night, because that's the only time I'm at peace.

My Silent Screams

Why is it so painfull? Why must I suffer like this? I feel like I'm not my own man because this illness has taken control of my life. Pain is seeing other people go on with their lives and it feels like you're stuck in parking. Pain is being in a room full of people and you still feel alone. Pain is seing other people laugh and you feel like you'll never be able to laugh like that again.

Living with this illness is like being dead among the living. It's so dark and you're trying to find the light but only darkness remains.

It feels like you're the only one hurting and feeling empty inside. It's like being under water and you can't breathe. It's so hard to catch your breath. I know I am not dead because I still have a dream and that is to one day be able to control this illness instead of it controlling me.

People are like flowers. We bloom and then we die. We are so fragile. When will I find peace inside my mind? This illness consumes me and it invades every space in my brain.

Oh! God, guide me in my time of need.

Now I know what people mean when they say that bad things happen to good people. At this moment I'm just tired of living with this illness.

It's crazy because it seems the pain will never let up. It feels like I'm being buried alive and I'm trying to dig my way out.

I have nothing to fear but fear itself.

Still I resist the pain, telling myself this illness is not worth dying for. There has to be a way out of this pit.

It's crazy the things this illness makes me think. Like asking my family and friends if I could take my own life. Asking them for permission. That's not fair for my family or for the people who care about me. All I know is that no matter what this illness makes me feel, I love all my family and friends. Mi mama, mis hermanos, mi sobrina, mi segunda familia, the Quintanilla family.

Remember guys, that no matter what happens to me I will always love you guys forever. It's unconditional love that I feel for you guys. You guys have been there for me through the good times and the worst of times.

It's a never ending story with this illness, the pain doesn't stop for even a second. I can't ever see straight. I feel I'm going blind. My eyes hurt. I feel like a prisoner inside my own mind.

Even through so much pain, I still have the good times when I was well. This illness can never take that away from me.

This illness is really pushing me to the limits of human endurance. Nobody really knows what is going on inside of me. This illness is really starting to scare me.

My world is totally different than the average person who is mentally well. I wish it would take me in my sleep so the pain and darkness could end. I really need a miracle. It's impossible for me to feel any worse than what I really feel. It's crazy but I already feel like I'm dead.

It's funny, to think I was once coming down with a physical illness. I wish it had been physical. At least I would have my sanity.

My Silent Screams

Been thinking today how this illness has simply turned my life completely around for the worst. I felt like I wasn't feeling like my old self. I remember I used to laugh. I can't remember the last time I laughed.

Will the rain last forever?

Will I ever see the world like I used to?

At the same time, though, this illness really got me close to my family. They know me intimately and that can never be taken away from me.

I'm just suffering too much. I can't see the way out of this. I feel like I'm on the other side of the fence where there is a merry-go-round and everybody is laughing and having a good time while I'm on the other side; the dark side. I am so uncomfortable being alive that it is just not fair. How could the human mind be closed down like if it was in a box? I'm stuck, please somebody help!

I know what Hell is like. It is dark and hot.

I know what the easy way out of this is. I won't do that because ever since I was born, life has never been easy. I've had to work hard for everything I have. Nothing has ever been given to me on a silver platter. I have always been a survivor.

Why can't I survive this illness?

Oh! God, get me out of my struggle! Master, do anything to take away the pain much faster.

A bright shiny day comes after the rain. The problems I'm having will go away because it's all gonna clear up after the rain.

The mountains I'm climbing will go away because a bright shiny day is right around the corner

I don't foresee any of that, but I must believe it. I need something to fight for to keep me alive.

Sometimes I Wonder

Another week gone by and I'm still not feeling better. It is so frustrating. What's the meaning of life? I still haven't found out yet.

I know it is not to be here on earth with this illness; that's just not fair.

Mental illness is like you're dying inside but outside you're looking fearless. While your tears are rolling down your face, you're still trying to hold on to what you have. It's crazy.

It seems the pain will never let up, but you still have to look for that light at the end of the tunnel.

───────────────────────────

This illness came to bring the pain hardcore to my brain. The worst time of my life is what I'm living through now. I feel like my legs are running but I'm still standing at the same spot. I feel like I'm screaming for help but my screams land on deaf ears. My mind, body, and soul long for a time of peace. Why does darkness engulf my whole being and doesn't let go? How long will it last; the torture of my mind, body and soul?

God, ease the pain and stop the crazy thoughts of suicide!

Journey Into Darkness

We are all God's children they say. But sometimes I wonder is there a God? Deep down in my heart I know there must be a God or else I wouldn't be here today.

Meanwhile, is there any hope in the midst of all this emptiness and sadness? I sometimes wonder how do I put up with all this pain? I wish I was a good artist so I could express my feelings through art.

Someday, I hope to control this illness and help other people who fall into the depths of this darknesss.

Today my friend Rick came to visit me. I was really glad to see him. We talked about what was going on with me. He told me that his girlfriend's son was going through a mental illness too. He is going to Maryland to get extensive testing on his brain.

I told him to get me some information because everything is free even the flight over there, he explained. Thats what I would like to do because I don't know what's going on inside of me.

I guess tomorrow is another day so *bring on the pain!*

I can take it. When I left Memorial Center I gave Lori a hug and told her in her ear "be strong." Now I have to apply the same wisdom to myself because sometimes I feel like I'm not going to make it. I can feel the Lord pulling, but He's pulling dead slow. While is this evil illness trying to make me commit the worst sin known to mankind? That is suicide! All I am is a single man. I can't be anybody but who I am now.

Sometimes I Wonder

This illness really humbles you to the core. I am living in my own world because my mind can't handle reality. It's amazing how much mental pain I'm putting my brain through. Man, I hate not being able to enjoy the beauty of life. I know I'm a Ruff Rider for putting up with this bullshit illness. How can I explain how I feel? Every time I wake up I feel a sickening feeling.

I refuse to give in to this illness.

Time seems to stop for me during the day. At night what I write in my jounal, I say to myself, "God, how time flies."

I was watching Selena the movie on T.V. and I realized that it has been 4 years since her untimely death. That's when I realized, Oh! God, how time really flies.

I look at myself in the mirror and I see such a humble man with so much pain inside. I look at myself and say, "You're a strong man, Pedro," as tears roll down my face. I look at myself and say, "God here I am still standing before you."

After I finished watching the movie, Selena, I got some inspriation to never give up on your dreams. Tomorrow is another day I guess. Every night I'm weary from battle, but I must go on.

There is no progress without struggle.

Either Let Me Fly or Give Me Death

Today I had a good day. I went to the fair with Marco and Jesse's family. At first I didn't want to go because I thought that I wouldn't enjoy myself. I figured that I would feel worse. But Jesse, being the true friend that he is, convinced me to go.

I'm so glad he did. I realized at the fair that there is so much beauty in life. And I think to myself how could those thoughts of suicide come into my head?

God, I would just like to thank you for today. I realize that what is happening to me is nothing new to this world. Many people have had this illness and it will continue happening to other people. I'm just one of those unfortunate ones who came down with this illness. This illness is either going to kill me or make make such a strong and spiritual person.

After I came back from the fair I sat on the side steps of my house and started crying uncontrollably. Because I thought to myself God there is so much living left for me to be done and I sometimes feel like quitting the game. I realized that I don't want this illness inside of me because I hate it. Unfortunately, it doesn't want to go anywhere. Tomorrow the sun will come up and we will see what happens.

Either Let Me Fly or Give Me Death

I see the world in a totally different way now. I don't take for granted every day that God gives me to live. I see kids as the best thing in the world. They are the ones who keep me going along with everyone who cares about me. Kids don't judge you they give you unconditional love.

That's why I have to keep going on no matter what. To see all the kids in my family grow up.

Please, God, give me strength to at least control this illness or even beat it.

Today is my brother, Tavo's birthday I told him happy birthday and shook his hand and gave him a big hug. I'm glad I was here to see my little brother turn 21.

God, turn my life around. This is enough suffering. I need to get on with my life. I've been living with this illness for far too long, I want to breathe freely again. Take the weight of the world off my shoulders. Let me walk on green pastures instead of all this glass and nails. Let me enjoy the endless beauty of this world. I'm in Hell but it doesn't scare me. I will fear no one while God is at my side.

Just sitting here hoping for better days.

I went to Dr. Walker's office today. He gave me confidence to try and control this illness. He told me to read a book called Mind Over Mood.

I've been feeling better these last couple of days. I thank God for that. I haven't had suicidal thoughts these last couple of days either. I feel that God is showing that pain is love. I have no evidence that I will be ill for the rest of my life and that gives me hope. I don't have evidence that I will have a wonderful life either, so I just have to take it day by day. The sun always comes out after this rain.

Lift my spirit, God, strengthen my soul and renew my mind. Open my heart to all the good things in life. Every day that goes by is a victory for me and a loss for the demons inside of me.

I don't want this pain any more. I want to be free from this enslaving illness. Run, Pedro, run because the demons are coming.

So I will keep on running until I reach my destination. Right now I feel like I can breathe again.

Oh! Thank you, God! I can't believe it took me 6 years to go back and get my high school diploma.

I ask you, Lord, to make me whole again. Living with this illness is good for nobody. I can feel myself feeling better little by little. Please, God, don't let this be another fluke.

Only God can judge me. We all must die but life goes on. Keep your head up, things will get brighter. I can't complain I was dealt this hell in life. I'm on this illness's most wanted list. I've taken everything this illness has dished out. I'm not scared because this illness has done all the damage it could do to me and I a still here standing strong. I've suffered so much, God, so shed your light on me. I just want to have those days when I can enjoy the laughter again. I'm just tired being in the darkness of this illness.

This illness really activates my hate toward Satan and all the evil in our world. All I know is pain, all I feel is rain.

Today I went to the doctor he said he was putting me back to work tomorrow. I just ask you, God, to help me control this illness so I can go back to work and function. I want my life back. Oh! God how I want my life back.

Either Let Me Fly or Give Me Death

Burning in Hell and I don't deserve to be. I might be alive in the flesh but I feel dead. You see I am not afraid of death but I just don't believe that suicide is the answer.

I feel like a caged-up animal. I know the worst pain in the world. I've been to the darkest depths of the mind. I'm going to hold on until what I have is gone. I wish that this illness would come out and face me.I would tear the fuck out of it. Let out all my anger, hate, frustration, and hopelessness.

I see the world in many shades of grays and blacks. God, can no one hear my silent screams? Was I born to lose or is this just a test? I know You keep me from going mad. It feels good to get away from the pain, it feels so good to get away from the rain.

What does this illness want from me? It doesn't want me to shine. It wants to keep me in the darkness. I refuse to give in. When I see myself in the mirror I can see and feel all that pain inside of me. No one can hear my silent screams.

Nobody can tell me that I haven't put my soul on the line to try and beat this illness. I will give it all I have to try and get to work.

Don't let this illness wear me out and make me feel like a one-hundred-year-old man. Help me to be strong, Lord.

Again, I feel like I'm going out of my mind. I feel like good and evil are pulling me apart. Feels like my body will give in and I will be torn apart. I'm slipping I'm falling and I can't get up. I gotta get up, gotta get back on my feet so I can tear shit up.

Now I cry but I shed no tears. My heart does the crying and sheds the tears. I just don't know what this illness wants from me. It made me have a horrible day at work.

I really need to learn how to control it. This illness will not take me under. I will fight it to the end. I still remember when I was a kid and I use to enjoy cartoons and just play and have fun. I just don't know what has a hold on me and it won't let go. Even though this illness did not let me sleep last night, I have to get some sleep tonight!

Fuck Satan!

God, bless me and let me keep going on. I just need to get away from the pain, stay away from the rain. I need the Holy Spirit to come down and ease my pain. I hope I get some sleep tonight.

Tomorrow is another day. This evil I have inside of me is driving me up the wall. How did it end up in what seems to be a dead end right in the pit of Hell?

Father, take my pain and turn it into joy. I'm just so sick and tired of feeling this way.

There seems to be no way out of this. God, just take this evil inside of me and destroy it. This illness doesn't do any good inside of me. Release me, Lord, release me.

Life is very cruel and there is nothing that anybody can tell me to convince me otherwise.

Whatever this evil does to me from here on out doesn't matter. Just keep my family safe. Give me pain until I die, but Father, please don't let this happen to anyone in my family, ever again.

I just need a place to rest but I just can't find it. I just need to get away from all this anxiety, depression and all this strain on my life.

Oh! God, why is it that I feel so much pain? I'm diving into the deepest darkest water is the world and I'm still going.

It's just so incredible what I've been through in what seems to be an eternity in Hell. I wish I had a release valve to release all the pain in my brain.

Tomorrow is another day to fight. Going to work makes me so fatigued and tired. It takes everything out of me. God I just don't know how much more of this I can take. Why am I suffering so much?

I have to be able to live with it. I know that its not my time to go yet. There has to be something, somewhere. This illnesss effects me on how I perceive time. There is no worst feeling in the world than this. I can't give up on myself. I'm a survivor.

I want to wake up some day and feel rested; feel re-energized. I haven't given up yet because I love my family so much. There is nothing I wouldn't do for my family.

God, take the pain, take the thoughts and dump them in the trash. The trash is where this illness belongs. It gets me sick to my stomach to feel this way.

When will this terrible nightmare of mine end? This illness has a hold on my mind but my heart and soul belong to God and my family. I feel trapped with nowhere to run, nowhere to hide. I can't get away from myself. It's just me against the world. Maybe it wasn't meant for me to be. I can't even relax for one second. Why? Oh! Why? I just don't know.

Take everything away from me; just give me my family and my mental health. What am I suppose to do? Where is hope; where is faith? I can't find them.

All that matters is that I'm still here. Why does it have to be such a hard struggle for me everyday? How can I maintain with so much on my brain? So many questions, not enough answers.

I'd love to go back to when we played as kids. This is such a lonely fight. I have all the support in the world and still nothing want to click inside my head. Will I even see the light?

I see my little puppy Lelo and he is so care free. I play with him and he doesn't realize how much pain I'm in.

Is there something evil inside of me? Why doesn't it let go?

Lord don't let go of me in my time of need. I'm tired of the strain and the pain. Am I suffering for nothing or will it payoff in the long run? The bottom of my feet ache so much from just working all day. What I'm going through right now is just so indescribable.

I love my family so much.

I'm running out of options at this moment.

There has to be something bigger than us out there.

I'm just going crazy.

How much more of the can I take? I made it to my 26th birthday. I really never saw myself making it this far. If I've made it this far I must keep going on.

Why can't I get away from this rain? The pain? I thank God for letting me see my 26th birthday, but what does the future beyond hold for me?

Going to work everyday is hell for me. When God asked for my story, I never thought it would be this dark and empty.

I feel like I'm losing control. Bring back the light in my eyes that I had when I was a kid.

Either Let Me Fly or Give Me Death

The saga continues.

I rebuke these thoughts, these feelings and all that I'm going through in the name of Jesus Christ.

When will it end? Nobody knows but God. Maybe I've always seen life differently than everyone else. Maybe this illness has been inside me of me since the beginning. But I must beat this evil that is inside of me no matter what.

Sometimes I feel like a monster who can't get out of my bubble. All these crazy thoughts inside of me and I can't get away from them! Oh! Mercy, mercy me, oh things ain't what they used to be.

What ever happened to all those blue skies and bright sunny days?

One thing that this illness cannot take from me is the love I have for my family and the love I have for the people who care for me. I can't forget the love I have for God. Even though there are days when I ask myself where are you, God, please show me the light in all this darkness.

If this illness doesn't kill me it can only make me stronger. I really am a survivor and there is no quit inside of me.

I have been working now for two weeks and I'm very proud of myself. Everything this illness makes me think is all lies from Satan and his evil plan to take as many souls to Hell as he can. But this is only the start of my spiritual warfare. I must continue to fight this evil. The war is going to be long and very painful. But what is pain to me, I know the worst pain in the world and I'm still going.

I just can't explain how much I love my family. They will always be in my heart no matter what happens to me. All I need now is God's Holy Spirit to come down and give me a place to rest inside of mind.

I need to elavate my spiritual being. God, please help me control this illness because it has taken advantage for far too long.

I really don't fear any evil, but sometimes the pain is so much that it feels like I'm going crazy. All I need, God, is for you to give me my second breath.

Sometimes I think to myself what is the point of me taking all this pain? But deep down inside my heart I know that God has a plan for me. I just wish that I could go to sleep and wake up in the morning feeling refreshed and full of life.

I know that I am still alive because my dream is still to one day wake up and be well again.

PUSH
Pray Until Something Happens

I am a true testamet of what the human spirit can endure.

I enjoy going to church on Sunday with Jesse's family. After church we go to Jesse's house and his wife cooks some very delicious food. I gain weight after I eat at their house.

The way I look at life is not pretty, but I know that there have to be better and brighter days ahead. I wish I could see clearly now. I wish I could see all obstacales in my way.

Either Let Me Fly or Give Me Death

No more pain. I don't want this evil inside of me any more.

I have so much love inside of me to offer this world. How can this illness tell me that there is nothing for me to live for? I refuse to comply with this illness because I have such a strong inner strength. This evil may control my mind, but my heart and soul belong to God.

I don't need money, fortune, or fame. All I need is my mental health. I don't desire anything from this world. All I desire is God. In the name of Jesus Christ, I rebuke Satan and all these thoughts and feelings of hopelessness.

There is so much beauty in this world that this illness doesn't let me experience it to the fullest. This illness really has a hold on me and it won't let go. I just want God to grab a hold on me and don't let go.

I probably always have been after the wrong things in life. There is nothing I can do about the past but I can do something about the future.

I don't want to spend one more day with this illness. In the midst of all this craziness there has to be something out there. In the midst of all this confusion I say to myself, "I can feel it coming in the air tonight, hold on. I've been waiting for this moment for all my life, hold on."

This is Hell and we are all here, can you feel it? It's in the air. Give me sight that I may recognize the evil in this illness.

Lord, why is it that I feel so much pain? All I see is black. All I feel is rain. God let me bask in your glory. Dealing with Satan is so hard.

Me, I'm all right I just have to work hard at it.

Lord, it started but when will it end?

Journey Into Darkness

No matter how long it lasts, I still thank you, Lord, for giving me my family. I am not perfect by a long shot. I confess to you daily. I come to you weak. All I ask for is strength. I can't loose sight of what I'm trying to do: beat this illness. What I'm going through right now is the biggest, hardest battle of my life.

God, grab a hold of me and don't let go. These dark clouds that hover over me are with me all day long.

What is it that makes me feel this way? I know that life can be a beautiful thing, that's why I keep hanging on for dear life. I want to live life to the fullest so bad.

God, just give me the strength and mental well-being so I can continue to work. My job is very important to me. I work with some good people.

There's no short cut home. I just let darkness creep into my soul. But I have such a strong desire that I feel my heart is on fire, trying to control this illness. I've gone the distance and I won't give up yet. Time keeps going on and it doesn't stop for anyone. Time heals all wounds. The strength that I have deep winthin me keeps the fire inside of me burning.

I thank God for the day I had today. I went to the movies with Ricky and Irene. We watched the movie Three Kings. The movie was pretty good.

After that, me and Ricky went to a dance club and danced with a woman named Gloria. I haven't danced in the longest time. So once again thank you, God for giving me the strength to do these things. I need to fill up this hole in my heart.

Either Let Me Fly or Give Me Death

God I thank you again for letting me have a good time in church today. God you have always been with me. I feel like I'm starting to wake up from the dead. I just thank you, God, for all the blessing that you have given me. As I write in this jounrla I have put my heart and soul into it. The fight is a long battle and I will be here until the end.

I thank you God for every breath I take in this lifetime. I'm finally starting to see the beauty of life which has always been there. I really feel so awesome. It's like I'm starting to see life the way is should be seen.

There is nothing in this earth I love more than mi familia. They are everything to me. They are my life. There is nothing I wouldn't do for my family. I want to break out of this darkness. I don't want it in my life anymore. I'm finally starting to enjoy life because some things are worth fighting for. There's no easy way out. I withstood everything this illness had to offer and I'm still standing strong. My heart is on fire for the desire to live.

I know that life won't be easy. But hopefully God will guide me that rest of the way. God may not be there when you call, but He's always on time.

A prayer from Mr. Earl Simmons, a.k.a DMX: I come to you hungry and tired and you give me food and let me sleep. I come to you weak you give me strength and that's deep. You call me a sheep and lead to green pastures only asking that I keep the focus in between the chapters. You give me the word and all that acts that I interpret and give me the eyes so that I could recognize the serpent.

You know I aint perfect but you'd like me to try and the devil who just wants me to lie till I die.

If It Takes for Me to Suffer

Lord, why is it that I feel so much pain?
All I saw was black all I felt was rain.
I come to you because it's you who knows.
You showed me that everything was black
Because my eyes were closed.

You let me bask in your glory
So it was only right that when you asked for this story
I put it together to help other people.
Plenty of times you sent help my way,

But I hid.

There was something that I just had to see
So I could be what you wanted me to be.
And I think I've seen it,
But I don't feel the same.

If It Takes for Me to Suffer

As a matter of fact I know I've seen it,
I can feel the change.
It's strange,
I thought I would never see the light.

But I've never known love like this before.
It's a wonderful feeling to get away from the pain,
And up under the ceiling to get away from the rain.

And the strain is gone, I feel.
I know what's real.
So I wipe away the tears.
I almost lost faith when I was in the realm of darkness.

And I feel that what I'm saying won't be heard until I'm gone.
But its all good because I really didn't expect to live long.
So if it takes for me to suffer for my brother to see the light,
Give me pain until I die.
But please, Lord, treat him right.

Amen.

Im Glad
An open-hearted prayer to God

God, you were just showing me that pain is love. Even though the devil was all over my face, I always stayed strong and prayed until the end.

I feel like I have so much love to give. I feel that my spirit is being uplifted. I thank you, God, for all the people you put in my life in my time of need.

This experience has taught me so much. I feel like I'm getting a second chance at life. The scars that this illness created in me will never go away, but I will never forget what I went through. The Lord's great mercy healed my soul. There is nothing I can be but a humble person. You always had a plan for me and it is starting to go into action.

I'm glad I never let go of your hand. You will be my guide from now until I die.

The weight of the world has been lifted off my shoulders. I can see clearly now.

I can see all obstacles in my way. My relationship with God has grown stronger. I have felt your Holy Spirit and He has taken away the fear. I can't thank you enough for being with me through the darknest episode of my life.

Im Glad

    I thank and love my family. I thank and love my second family the Quintanilla's and everyone who cares about me. I pray that God looks after us in our stay here on earth. All praise and glory go to you, Father God, because without you I am nothing.

    With Love,
    Your Creation.

In the Darkest of My Days

In the darkest days of my illness, I have always wanted to kill myself, because of all the nonstop mental pain. Now that I feel better, my views on the world have changed.

All I have to do is figure them out on my own.

Sometimes I feel like I've lost my soul in this fight I put up with this illness. I will never forget the darkest hours this illness made me go through.

I remember thinking that I would never get out of my own horror show. Imagine screaming at the top of your lungs for help!

And nobody can hear you. I takes another madman to hear my silent screams. Now that I know that Hell does exist, I don't want to go there.

All I have to say is fuck Satan! Fuck all his demons and fuck all of Hell! Satan is the most coward ass bitch that there ever was and that there will ever be. Fuck the world if they don't shun Satan. Yes, I'm crazy. You have to be crazy to live in this messed up world we live in, but crazier to go along with the kind of world Satan wants it to be.

I'm willing to die for what I believe in. I'm willing to die for what I know is truth. I will fear nobody or anything and love only God.

In the Darkest of My Days

    I will die in order for my family to live a better life. Like Tupac Shakur said, "I've got nothing to loose; it's just me against the world."

    We all pay for what we do in this world. There is nobody in this world who can take what God has given me or what He's going to give me.

    And that's real.

I See Life a Little Differently Now

I never knew a love like this before.
Life is a blessing now;
You've got me smiling from inside of my heart
When inside it was dark
And it doesnt rain anymore.
Only sunshine;
No pain anyomore,
I really love mine.

You washed away the tears
And the fears.
And I'm happy now
More than I've ever been in my life
The whole twenty-eight years.
That's fromt he heart.
To live is to suffer and to survive
Well that's to find meaning in the suffering.

I See Life a Little Differently Now

People who know me
Know that I'm a survivor.
One thing that I've learned from this experience
Is that pain is Love.
I've seen darkness and Hell at a glance.
No matter how hard it rains,
Withstand the pain.

Never give up!
Tough guys don't stay down long!

The Reason

The reason I am sharing this journal is to let people know how painful it is to live with bipolar disorder.

I originally started writing this journal as a suicide note in a paper notebook. Then I decided that no matter how hard it gets to live with depression, there is no reaosn to take one's own life.

I hope that by someone reading this journal, they realize that they are not alone, there are too many people in the world who suffer from some sort of mental illness. Someone once wrote that "To live is to suffer. To survive, well, that's to find meaning in the suffering."

I just hope that my pain is not in vain. That there is a reason for all my suffering. Everyday I pray to God that He, by some miracle, heal me of my illness. Then the realization came to me that I'm going to have to live with this illness for the rest of my life.

I realize that after living with this ailment for eight years, all I can do is fight it all the way until the end of my life.

The Reason

I see a doctor and take medication to maintain my sanity in this crazy world. One thing I do know is that this illness is in my D.N.A. I was born with it. It's in my genetics. It was given to me by someone in my family from past generations. I just hope that if there is life after death, I make it into the gates of Heaven for all my suffering. Someone once told me that we are not given a soul, but we have to find it through pain and suffering.

The worst thing about bipoar disorder, is the depression.

I realized that I'm going to be a tortured soul from now until the day that I die. The fight between God and Satan for my soul will last till my death. I know that spiritual warfare, the fight between good and evil, will continue until the end of humanity.

Sometimes I start crying for no reason, but I realize that I cry for the world. I feel like the weight of the world is on my shoulders. I feel like the pain and suffering of the world is inside of me. Because I have a great relationship with God. I have a good family and I don't wish for the things of this world. So I feel like I should not have a reason to suffer or cry as I do for no reason.

To tell you the truth, I don't know much about religion, but I do believe in God, and I will walk with him for the rest of my life. I just wish the Lord would come down from Heaven and show humanity how to live, and we could have peace of earth. No more hunger, no more killings…

But then I remember what He said in the person of Jesus Christ, that the knowledge of how to live and love is already written in our hearts.

What we need to do is replace hate with love, evil with good, and so on.

Every night before I go to sleep, I pray for humanity, peace on earth, and for mother Earth, and everything God created on her. I always talk to Him.

He doesn't talk back, but I have all the faith in the world that He listens to my prayers and the prayers of humanity.

This experience hasn't killed me so it must make me stronger.

One of God's son's,
Pedro Ramirez

God Loves you.
God Loves you.

www.ingramcontent.com/pod-product-compliance
Lightning Source LLC
Chambersburg PA
CBHW050606300426
44112CB00013B/2098